Jo Shapcott was born in London. Poems from her three collections, *Electroplating the Baby* (1988), *Phrase Book* (1992) and *My Life Asleep* (1998) are gathered in a selected poems, *Her Book* (2000). She has won a number of literary prizes including the Commonwealth Writers' Prize for Best First Collection, the Forward Prize for Best Collection and the National Poetry Competition (twice). *Tender Taxes*, her versions of Rilke's French poems, was published in 2001.

In the Faber & Faber 90th anniversary series

T. S. Eliot – *The Waste Land* (1922)
Marianne Moore – *Selected Poems* (1935)
W. H. Auden – *Another Time* (1940)
Ted Hughes – *The Hawk in the Rain* (1957)
Sylvia Plath – *Ariel* (1965)
Philip Larkin – *High Windows* (1974)
Seamus Heaney – *The Haw Lantern* (1987)
Wendy Cope – *Serious Concerns* (1992)
Daljit Nagra – *Look We Have Coming to Dover!* (2007)
Jo Shapcott – *Of Mutability* (2010)

JO SHAPCOTT

Of Mutability

FABER & FABER

First published in 2010
by Faber & Faber Ltd
Bloomsbury House
74–77 Great Russell Street
London WC1B 3DA
This edition first published in 2019

Typeset by Faber & Faber Ltd
Printed in England by CPI Group (UK) Ltd, Croydon, CR0 4YY

A CIP record for this book is available from the British Library

ISBN 978–0–571–35235–7

2 4 6 8 10 9 7 5 3 1

Acknowledgements

Acknowledgements are due to the editors of the following
publications: *After Pushkin*, *Guardian*, *Independent*, *Poetry*
(U.S.), *Poetry London*, *Poetry Review*, *The Times*. I would
like to give my warmest thanks to the following organisations
for their support: the Barbican, the Calouste Gulbenkian
Foundation, the City of London Festival, the Civitella Ranieri
Foundation, the Laurence Sterne Trust, the Presteigne Festival,
the Royal Philharmonic Society, the Society of Authors, and
the Poetry Archive where recordings of some of these poems
appear. My thanks also to the composers John McCabe and
John Woolrich for working with my words, and to the neuro-
scientist Mark Lythgoe who, for the poem 'Composition',
introduced me to latent inhibition (the ability we have to filter
out irrelevant stimuli).

The artist Helen Chadwick is the presiding spirit of this
collection. Many of the poems, including 'The Oval Pool'
and 'Piss Flower', refer directly or indirectly to her work.
I am also indebted to Marina Warner's illuminating writings
about her.

This book owes everything to Dr Sam Guglani, Dr Sean
Elyan and their team at Hereford County Hospital.

Contents

OF MUTABILITY

Of Mutability

Too many of the best cells in my body
are itching, feeling jagged, turning raw
in this spring chill. It's two thousand and four
and I don't know a soul who doesn't feel small
among the numbers. Razor small.
Look down these days to see your feet
mistrust the pavement and your blood tests
turn the doctor's expression grave.

Look up to catch eclipses, gold leaf, comets,
angels, chandeliers, out of the corner of your eye,
join them if you like, learn astrophysics, or
learn folksong, human sacrifice, mortality,
flying, fishing, sex without touching much.
Don't trouble, though, to head anywhere but the sky.

Era

The twenty-second day of March two thousand and three
I left home shortly after eight thirty
on foot towards the City. I said goodbye
to the outside of my body: I was going in.
The magpies were squabbling in the park.
The little fountain splashed chemical bubbles
over its lip. Traffic swarmed and swam
round Vauxhall Cross, like crazy fish, with teeth.

And anything could be real in a country
where Red Kites were spreading east and now
we had February swallows. Planes for Heathrow
roared not far enough overhead, shedding
jet trails which pointed over there: those other
places where all the frontiers end with a question.

La Serenissima

I was on land, but the land didn't belong
to earth any more, was allowed to rest
in floating patches here and there.
The pavement rippled under my shoes.
Everything I could see belonged to water:
liquid churches, theatres, monuments, houses,
liquid sun and sky. My hands wandered
into water, cupped water. My face turned

towards rainclouds. I could feel the membranes
in my body tremble with the fluid
they contain, and the stately flow of lymph,
the faster pulse of blood. A boat's engine
vibrated through land, through waves, through my feet
into my torso. Slow – slowly moving, I stepped on.

Deft

It's as easy to make an antibubble in your own kitchen
as it is to open up a crease in language

and reveal what you couldn't say yesterday.
Just a matter of squirting water onto water

without snapping the surface tension until liquid
surrounds a skin of air, surrounding liquid. My body's

a drop of water. Maybe the imperfections, the proliferating cells
help it refract the full spectrum. These last breaths,

air, water bubbling at my lips. The soap film is my skin:
permeable-for-some-things, membrane, separating-other-things,

this and that, the moving point between, the unsettled
limit, stretching and contracting under the breath

that comes and goes: I am this one, I am that one,
I breathe in and become everything I see.

The Oval Pool

All that's left are a dozen copies of my elastic self in blue,
molecules trapped in time, my image – arching, breathing,

prone – across a dry and azure pool. There will be no evaporation.
My twelve blue selves embody our contract with pleasure, sing

the hymn of praise for impurity. I was semi-permeable.
One copy holds a mirror. Everyone around me's weeping,

addressing themselves to five gold spheres, bubbles in which
they can see the tears that may be theirs. Every still life should

showcase animals: here trapped gas has rounded the belly of the lamb
and even photocopying shows the film over the fish's eye.

In death they whirl and fly in my Xerox arms: a goose, herrings,
a crab, two mice, a skate, three rabbits, a starfish, rats and a squid,

bouncing on the copy surface tension of the oval pool,
all of us blowing and blown under the sticky water,

circling in the blue dry solution, circling
in the gorgeous mess of our own gravity.

Hairless

Can the bald lie? The nature of the skin says not:
it's newborn-pale, erection-tender stuff,
every thought visible – pure knowledge,
mind in action – shining through the skull.
I saw a woman, hairless absolute, cleaning.
She mopped the green floor, dusted bookshelves,
all cloth and concentration, Queen of the moon.
You can tell, with the bald, that the air
speaks to them differently, touches their heads
with exquisite expression. As she danced
her laundry dance with the motes, everything
she ever knew skittered under her scalp.
It was clear just from the texture of her head,
she was about to raise her arms to the sky;
I covered my ears as she prepared to sing, to roar.

Riddle

I am always behind
or on top of you.
Full of dust, ash, and air
I smell of every room
you ever walked through.
I rise when offended,
creak when wet. How
easily we part, adieu,
how often I leave trails
of myself in your wake.

Abishag

after Rilke

I

Tie my arms round the neck
of my beloved, so as to wrap
me close, even when I'm asleep
through long, sweet hours of wedlock

with my face in his beard,
the hair so thick owls might nest
where my cheek nests and those be small bird
cries, not the sound of my dearest

wheezing. Stars tremble in his sweat
though he feels cold. I lick his skull
dry. My own perfume stirs, stinks abject
and rose against the enormous other smell.

I can feel his mind through my tongue
as I trace patterns with the tip across his scalp.
The curtain flutters, I hear a tiny owl yelp
in his throat. They sponge us down as one.

II

All day my beloved is empty in his chair.
He tries to tell me what he's done, and hasn't felt
so far, of his dog and his life as an angler.
I want the night when I'm the author
of what time's left to us and only his dear
old man's skin between us, so thin it might melt
against my breasts under the hot quilt.

On and off his knowledge of women seeps back,
his eyebrows knot and he's remembering – a trick
or two, some little nibble, or touch, what my mouth
is for – though he's not doing. I smile and hold him
like my own child, a precious child whose birth
was at least as hard as his death, his dear, soon death
will be. Something stirs, somewhere in the room.

The Deaths

I thought I knew my death.
I thought he would announce
himself with all the little creaks
and groans you hear of,
that we'd get friendly and walk
our walk of two drunkards
with him chattering inside me
about lumps and arteries
and his gift of pain which would be
too big to wrap properly,
that some way into our courtship
he'd give me the look and
I'd implode like a ripe mango.

I thought I knew my death
so when, after a bee buzz
of an afternoon, the rain started
and the fine hairs rose on my neck
and the long hairs tugged my scalp
and my mouth stank of seaweed
and a tingle ran round my wrists,
I didn't recognise her. She lit
a green flame over my head
and even then I didn't get it. She threw
me yards back, traced her filigree
red cartoons on my palms until
I was gone and still I didn't know.

Scorpion

I kill it because we cannot stay in the same room. I kill it because we cannot stay in the same room with me sleeping. I kill it because I might look away and not see it there on the wall when I look back. I kill it because I might spend all night hunting it. I kill it because I am afraid to go near enough with glass and paper to carry it outside. I kill it because I have been told to. I kill it by slapping my shoe against the wall because I have been told to do it that way. I kill it standing as far away as possible and stretching my hand holding the shoe towards it. I kill it because it has been making me shake out the bedclothes, look inside my shoes, scan the walls at night. I kill it with two fast blows in case one isn't enough. I kill it because I can. I kill it because it cannot stop me. I kill it because I know it is there. I kill it so that its remains are on the heel of my shoe. I kill it so that its outline with curved sting is on my wall. I kill it to feel sure I will live. I kill it to feel alive. I kill it because I am weaker than it is. I kill it because I do not understand it. I kill it without looking at it. I kill it because I am not good enough to let it live. I kill it out of the corner of my eye, remembering it is black, vertical, stock still on the white wall. I kill it because it will not speak to me.

Religion for Girls

Just now, we need as many as we can get.
Myself, I'd like an underground goddess
to supervise the tube, to watch the drains.
A god for airlines, one for dodgy builders
and one for children's breath. But we've got this,
a temple filled with marble body parts:
the giant hand with which Mithras killed the bull;
Minerva's head, her helmet lost, her wisdom
leaking out; a tiny Mercury too small to dash
between earth and paradise, stuck chatting here;
a local London genius for this and that;
an elderly god for the Thames, lying down;
a mother goddess, unnervingly, powerfully plump;
a god from Egypt for the underworld;
Bacchus for giving sparky life. And all,
all of these gods and bits of gods left here
to chew over the wandering mortals of London,
as we chant our *Evening Standard*s to ourselves
in our stalled commuter trains, curse under breath
at traffic jams, high rises, shopping centres
and go about our business following
the invincible sun from east to west.

Religion for Boys

Thursday night in the temple of Mithras
is busy. Deals to do, rituals to keep,
favours to return. But all the lads
take time to nod to the goddess as they go,
the little stone figure in the porch
who overflows on to her plinth. No female's
been through that church door, not even her,
more ancient than the altar carved like a movie
where a sacred bull has an ear of corn sprouting
from his tail, and a raven, dog, snake and scorpion
surround the young god under the sun and moon.
She's older than resurrection and she's seen
it all before. The men, muttering and striving
before the sacrifice, eyeing each other's rank.
She chuckles. These boys do such hard graft,
big tests where they're sat hard against the fire
torturing themselves through seven grades towards
perfection. The costumes – and the drinking,
whether beer, wine or cockerel blood,
it starts them chanting Father! Father! Father!
the word sliding out of the temple, through
the porch, into the goddess's granite fists
until she lets it fly to the sun and to the moon.

The Death of Iris

He paces the garden, hunting in the borders
where nothing's in the right place. A shrub
growing small harmoniums: that can't be true.
And what are they doing there, those flowers
with the faces of bereaved dogs and scared kittens?
Bindweed, made of paperwork and damp beer mats,
is flourishing in the shadows but what's needed
now is a spot in sunlight most of the day.

Find it, dig deep, because the picture on the packet
shows it'll look great, bloom a good part of the year;
the flower is the colour her soul has traced
in the eyes of those left behind, the colour
in the sixth band of the rainbow
she lets us glimpse every now and then.

St Bride's

There is a tower of the winds as tall
as this one in another city, a steeple
filled with fire by the incendiary raids
of a coalition of the unwilling. Nocturnal
shocks pound the citizens who survive,
blast them out of their beds into the streets,
children bundled under their arms. The gutters flame.
Dust is alight. I was born in a city

to come and go safely through the boroughs,
carrying inside me every morning's news: pictures
of soldiers in places they didn't want
to understand, made to fight for loose change,
for the hell of it, for a can of oil. I live here,
the smell of print and ashes in my nose.

Sinfonietta for London

A garden that's a building that's a garden.
Walk under the glass beacon and step
on to a carpet of octandrous flowers.

The walls have lungs and eyelids
and fins of glass, and fins of limestone
to conduct us through the city air.

Pass through its many densities of stone,
glass, metals, and learn to stroll for once,
no avant-garde: only all of us slight behind.

Integral are the living sounds of Fenchurch Street,
the mechanised city with its patterns
of soft and loud, its winds

and echoes a totally open musical space,
full of people with their unsuspected sounds
and their parallel routes through traffic

and your darling's head floating
above the rest, singing and whistling
all the way down to the Thames.

Gherkin Music

walk the spiral
                up out of the pavement
        into your own reflection, into
transparency, into the space

                where flat planes are curves
        and you are transposed
as you go higher into a thought

                of flying, joining the game
        of brilliance and scattering
where fragments of poems,

                words, names fall like glory
        into the lightwells until
St Mary Axe is brimming

La Canterina

I can spring as high
        and nimbly as a flea;
                and I can execute
twenty entrechats
        in sequence
                without pausing
for breath,
        at each leap
                clicking my heels
eight times:
        I can do the same
                for all the entrepas
and I swear
        I make even the best
                of all the rest
a block of stone.
        I like to add
                a detail or two
to any complex
        dancing
                sometimes juggling
or often a song
        mystical and remote
                to split the mood.
Performing
        on a tightrope
                makes me feel wanton –
all the space
        underneath
                and the swaying

and the dazzle
        of my own steps.
                They jostle
to see my legs
        from below
                and I might
croon stars at them,
        the moon at them if I like.
                I love it
when they believe
        in me, half-naked
                technical,
distressed,
        and showing off
                at the top of my voice.

Shapcott's Variation on Schoenberg's Orchestration of Bach's Prelude and Fugue in E♭ major, 'St Anne'

Where does it come from this passion
for layers? I could eat the lexicon,
breathe whole fugues in German and Latin,
rub notes on my skin to make the pores sing.

I love it, like this, when I lose touch
with whose the voice is, whose the fingers
on the bow, the pen, whose mouth
the noise belongs to in the end.

Numbers make me tremble in spring.
I want to counterpoint them until I careen
off the edge of the world disputing
with God himself about the number seven.

The Black Page

The page opens
its dark portrait
of a rectangular mouth
and says believe
in alas. Believe
in mourning and
a proper afterlife
which you will come
to understand once
you strip off, fall in
and swim in ink.

The Gypsies' Tales of Ovid
after Pushkin

There's a story still doing the rounds:
the Roman Emperor once deported a man
from the South, sent him here into exile with us.
I used to know, but have forgotten his odd name.
He was old under his skin, had always been,
but his soul was young and shivering with life
so that everything he touched turned into song
and his voice was like the sound of rushing water.
And we all loved him here with us, living
on the banks of the Danube, no bother,
no side to him, charming us with stories.
We found his understanding of what's what tiny,
a child he was, helpless and shy, a baby.
Imagine, needing strangers to catch your game
and net and gut your fish, do all your basics.
When the fast river froze itself into stone
and the winds swept in from the north
they covered him – smooth as a saint he was underneath –
with fluffy fur, rabbit, squirrel and fox.
Small chance he'd take to our poor way of life,
our different worries: hunger, dance and touch.
He wandered around, skin pale and heart dried up,
telling who'd ever listen about some god
who'd singled him out to punish for a mistake.
He was waiting for a change of heart upstairs.
He grieved out loud, thought warm thoughts about death,
every daylight minute, paced beside the Danube,
shouted at the ice, watched his tears drop, steaming,
yelled words to himself about his home, his city.

Dying he heated up, boiling with words;
he cursed and screamed instructions about his bones
which he swore were pulling south inside him.
They at least should be allowed to leave
to carry some grains of his soul back to the world.

Aleko

after Pushkin

I called him my little cuckoo,
always on the edge, pushing,
passing through, no nesting instinct,
afraid to get used to anything.
Everywhere, to him, was open road –
even the track of my fingertip
on his skin – everywhere a pillow.
Mornings he'd give the day up to his god
of the moment, hoping that way to stop
the ordinary shocks of life
disturbing his pulse. Sometimes fame,
the magic of success, that far-off star
would lure him. The sort of luxury
and expensive fun he never expected
fell into his lap from time to time.
He was alone, with the thunder rumbling above him,
more than once, but he slept on under storms,
rows upstairs, loud flight paths, slept on under
blue quiet ceilings. He knew the fates
were depicted blind, designing,
but he took no more notice than a fingerclick,
though God knows, passion
had made a trampoline of his soul
had raged through his torso
like an invading army.
He thought he could control even that.
He'll wake up though. Wait.

His 'n' Hers

He was starting to feel buff
what with all the selenium.
Those days vitamins and minerals
flew onto his tongue like the host
every morning, so many tablets
you'd think his cells had shares
in GlaxoSmithKlein. He'd been
raiding his assets too long, allowing
strength to drip out in some
byzantine effort to be as all-knowing
as a space telescope, tight-arsed
and satisfied with the tiny kernel
he knew his brain to be.

She wanted to run away with him,
text him from only feet away
and work towards their reincarnation
into each other. They'd hide out
in the damp, waiting for the beading
to bend away from the wall and when
Christ's face appeared in the skirting,
she knew the markets would crash,
the financial ripples would leave marks
on their bodies, in fact, spreadsheets
summarising the whole shit storm.

Somewhat Unravelled

Auntie stands by the kettle, looking at the kettle
and says, help me, help me, where is the kettle?
I say, little auntie, the curlicues and hopscotch grids
unfurling in your brain have hidden it from you. Let me
make you a cup of tea. She says ah ha! but I do
my crossword, don't I, OK not the difficult one, the one
with the wasname? Cryptic clues. Not that. I say,
auntie, little auntie, we were never cryptic
so let's not start now. I appreciate your straight-on talk,
the built-up toilet seats, the way you wish poetry
were just my hobby, our cruises on the stair lift,
your concern about my weight, the special seat in the bath.
We know where we are. She says, nurse told me I
should furniture-walk around the house, holding on to it.
I say, little auntie you are a plump armchair
in flight, a kitchen table on a difficult hike without boots,
you do the sideboard crawl like no one else, you are a sofa
rumba, you go to sleep like a rug. She says,
I don't like eating. Just as well *you've* got
a good appetite. I say littlest auntie, my very little auntie
(because she is shrinking now, in front of me)
let me cook for you, a meal so wholesome and blimmin'
pungent with garlic you will dance on it and
eat it through your feet. Then she says don't you
ever want to go to market and get lost
in pots, fruit and random fabric? Don't you
want to experiment with rain, hide out in storms,
cover your body with a layer only one raindrop
thick? Don't you want to sell your nail-clippings
online? She says, look at you, with all your language,

you never became the flower your mother
wanted but it's not too late, come with me
and rootle in the earth outside my front window,
set yourself in the special bed, the one only
wasname is allowed to garden and we will practise
opening and closing and we'll follow the sun
with our faces until the cows come home.

Tea Death

When he passed out into his tea
he expected to wake up with his nose
warm and wet, lungs topped up
with Earl Grey, snorting

tea leaves which would gather
in the distant networks
of his blood. It might be a relief
to drown that way and not

in the fine wine he'd ploughed
an expert front crawl through
all these years. At tea time.
Splashing through Lapsang

towards scones even angels
fought over, where the Earl himself
would face him at table,
and they'd grin at each other

so hard that golden liquid
would strain through their teeth,
leak out under their nails,
from their ears, tear ducts, nipples

and then – if they laughed –
spout from their wobbling
belly buttons like the outward
breaths of whales.

The Bet

I wanted to stay awake longer than
anyone else in our student house.
I wanted to beat them all at not sleeping.
In my room I stocked up on fruit, nuts,
and herbal teas. I kept a diary.

Eleven hours forty-six minutes:
'The hardest part is staying in one place.'
I trained my mind for wakefulness,
talked to the others through the door.

Twenty-eight hours thirty-two minutes:
'Speech hopping and skipping, colours so bright
they appear, very. Another near-sleep experience.'

Thirty-six hours seventeen minutes:
'Crashed out of my own head into the centre
of this book, this diary. I miss dreaming.'

All Flesh Is

When the glass roof shattered over my desk,
little cubes pitted my laptop, settled
ankle-deep on the rug. Silicon dust flew inside
and outside my clothes: I tasted it on my lips.
I swept and dusted, bore off a ton of fragments,
the heart of each piece milky blue in the light –
O alchemy of self-cleanness and therms.
I breathed glass, it settled in my hair.
I felt fine grit in my sheets that night,
in my sleep, and out of it, when I stirred.
I woke up to bare sky over my books,
my flesh was glass, I spoke in little clicks
and chinks, and my transparent self
went about its business all that day, the usual.

Alternative

She rolled the small jade marble into her ear.
It would do her good, relieve her somniphobia –
though she wasn't sure it was a bad thing
to stay awake: she wanted more of this time,
this conscious time. Sleepers lie on their backs,
hands crossed on their chests, missing it all.
The marble was cool in her ear canal, it rustled
against her eardrum when she moved.
She thought it would fly out, with a palm-pat,
after the prescribed hour. She tilted her head,
knocked her skull with her palm, jumped
on the spot, touched her toes, poked it with a straw,
poked it with the end of spoon, soaped her little
finger. A toothpick. She made a lasso with dental floss
and tweezers, tried suction with a latex glove.
The toy submarine on a string was next.
She sent in a hummingbird: the wings tickled,
he knocked the jade with his beak. The kitten
wouldn't put his paw into the dark of her head,
the snail was too slow to bear. The grass snake
dozed in the auditory curve. It went on for
three days and three nights non-stop, until
some dark time passed, an accidental sleep
of stone lapping ear bones, wavelets of marble,
then she raised her head from the bathroom floor
and jade rolled into her open hand.

Night Flight from Muncaster

Reader, you're an owl
for this moment, your flower-
face a white scrawl
in the dark, a feather frill.

Feel a pair of flat
cheeks grow, satellite
dishes to funnel sound,
not to transmit, sweet

hungry noises, to ears set
uneven for range. You'll hear best
if you tilt and jerk your head, blast
it towards the smallest rattle of dust.

You're an owl from your raptor
talons to your huge eyes which sculpt
a deep, narrow path through the night:
check how close together they've crept

for depth perception. And feathers,
adapted for silence on the wing.
And now you're flying as fast as slang,
as quiet as the moment after a song.

Below is a sandstone ravine where you harness
updrafts, try out some height then swoop low
past the aerial walkway to disgorge a pellet
for a child to find and keep for her project.

Rare for a barn owl to fly to the sea shore
but you want to feel and test every feather,
enjoy the tug of wing-muscles, stir
your way through miles and miles of sheer air.

That's how you find yourself at North Berwick,
preening by the harbour, well back
from thousands of seabirds on islands and rocks
who live for clamour, for the noise of the flock

so that even late at night
your auriculars catch chat enough
to block out the quiet.
But up to this minute

you've been learning
how to read the silences of air,
its meanings, currents and pressures.
You can hear clouds creak, droplets hiss.

Border Cartography

I *Arbeia*

Here the earth tells its story
to the sea, the sky;
the estuary in between
leaks history.

We're listening so hard
but the wind hereabouts
whips up its own
noisy version of the truth.

II *Carrawburgh*

The sky's so big
you'd like to trace
God's design in the palm
of your hand for safety.

Instead local deities compete
noisily for the honour
of catching the sun
in their nets as it passes.

III *Carlisle*

Towers, walls, the castle –
even the earth we measure
with our steps on this walk –
are tough as you like.

In this light, the red stone
is more tender than stubborn:
the castle keep gifted
with the surface of a peach.

IV *Castell Dyserth*

There's a fish mountain
not far from here, crammed
with antediluvian bones.
This hillock is smaller,

the stones raided,
only the ground
wanting to remember
the fragments it's made of.

v *Montgomery*

It's like being inside a shell
the way the hills encircle
the town. And the rain's
made mother-of-pearl

of the streets. The font
in the church is so old
that just to touch it brings
drizzle down from the west.

vi *Sedbury Cliffs*

How many strange secrets
have we told the insects
on the muddy cliff top?
Armies of wood lice and spiders

skitter across fossils
of bivalves and ammonites.
There are other risks: gaze
down the estuary at the chemical sea.

I Go Inside the Tree

Indoors for this ash
is through the bark;
notice its colour –
asphalt or slate in the rain –

then go inside, tasting
weather in the tree rings,
scoffing years of drought and storm,
moving as fast as a woodworm

who finds a kick of speed
for burrowing into the core,
for mouthing pith and sap,
until the O my god at the heart.

My Oak

has memory: it put the wind which shook
the sapling into the mass of its trunk;
it put the prevalence of weather
down Hanter Hill into its weighted curve
across the skyline; that infestation
of caterpillars was remembered by the leaves
which contracted and thickened the next year.
It remembers the seasons, or at least the length
of darknesses which distinguish them:
our word is photoperiodism, but remember
is not the word, nor is it my oak although
I used to watch it every day, when
I lived across the field, watch it
respond to everything, everything else.

Cedar of Lebanon

Not for climbing, its branches
are spread in flat planes
for maximum solar exposure,
scraggy underneath and green
melting into blue-green on top.
I do not know it, over there across the valley.
I cannot smell the sap from here,
nor think of it as mystical or healing.
I do not know why I want to speak
about vertical grooves and dark bark
the colour of elephant hide
or cracked pony, when it is not so.

Trasimeno Olive

Long breaches make air spiral
as tangibly as the heartwood.
It's only human to think the olive
speaks, that there are mouths
singing, screaming, even, in the gashes
and you can't help but see a figure
twined in the trunk or struggling out.
Layers of xylem and crushed phloem
are other ways we see 'tree':
there are always these speaking
gaps to put a fist in or a heart.

Cypress

Visit it in the dark. Cicadas
are inside your head as your hand
reaches towards bark: you feel
the latent heat first then the surface,
scabbed with lichen you can't see
but know from the fizz where touch
meets memory. Before all this,
the scent, which is anti-language
(only, as it drifts into your body
the words slip in, as well),
and made of earth, air, sun
and human consciousness.

Shrubbery

What's that in the privet,
hurtling around the branches
and dead leaves? It's one
of my spare hands, grubbing
through the bramble
for blackberries. It's my old
trainers, dancing now they
are free of my feet. It's my
poor little auntie tugging
at the twigs of her dementia.
It's me, spinning inside
the brown foliage, laughing
and blink-squinting at every
here-gone, here-gone, here-gone
glimpse of the sun.

For Summer

The lie is light over your heart.
You will do nothing about it.
The swallows are chattering
around the house. All night
you sweat it out waiting for a breeze
to collapse you to sleep.

You lay down in front of your door,
your head pointing north, but
none of the other cardinal points
creep into your body. Your ears,
loosened with olive oil, tune into
difficult stars, loud and hot.

Summer is going. You are already
running into the first snowflake,
mouth open to taste it, primed
to ingest all the weathers.

Where I Worked

Prickle of bramble, damsons
twitching in the wind, a tiny shed
in a field corner, its window
red in the sunrise, the smell
of grass as I run towards it,
arms up as if to stir the sky.
My fingerprint has dented
the whole hillside so the stream
will never run the same course again.

Forecast

A cloud sat on the hill all August
until the sun was a ghost memory
and the fields were full of water,
the ground an unlicked sponge.
When the sun came out at last,
in October, she lost it, beat her head
against her unfamiliar shadow
on the wall, her voice, but not her voice,
chanting over and over, 'It's a sad child
that destroys its own weather.'

Viral Landscape

I went outside and found the landscape
which had eaten my heart. I will lose
my mean-time, and spruce and eye-water.
The field was just mown and the summer

so hot there was no green in it,
layers of russets and yellows,
and I was swelling with mosquito
bites, and I was listening to Fado.

The trees around the perimeter
were a block of solid colour,
(my stomach fluttered at the sight – and
gut epithelium is five days old at most)

shockingly uni-green by contrast.
Look further into the stands of trees
and everything changes (my cerebral
and visual cortex is as old as me). The eye

can't locate an individual shade:
it's all delicate tips and hints
of green rolling in the wind.
We are moving and I can't see a thing.

Myself Photographed

So this is me. In the field after we got lost.
My eyes are turned up to the right
and my mouth is a little open.
Perhaps I always look like this.
Perhaps it is an expression of surprise
that I am in the world at all, let alone
that this wrong turning resulted in an oak
(I want to say leaf, leaf); high grass (I want
to say hay tickle); my dodgy ankle (I want to
say friendly old pain); the warm tang
of saliva in my mouth (I want to say
charged tongue); my body cells
so new, fresh, and not disorderly at all
(I want to say Hope) and O the weather there
which was hot, so hot, so hot, so hot that day.

Uncertainty is Not a Good Dog

Uncertainty is not a good dog.
She eats bracken and sheep shit,
drops her litters in foxholes
and rolls in all the variables,

wriggling on her back until
she reeks of them,
until their scents are her scents.
She takes sudden, windy routes

through hummocks, cairns and ditches
so you can't spot where she is
and acknowledge her velocity
at the same time. She's fidgety,

but still careful to snuffle
through all the mud on the trail.
She can't see in the dark
but bumps her snout

on the overhang lapping
the path. Daylight's no better:
she has to screw her eyes
tight against the glare

and, panting, just risk it, following
her nose across the landscape,
her tongue brighter than probability,
brighter than heather, winberry and scree.

Composition

And I sat among the dust motes, my pencil
(blue) sounding loud on the page, and
a blast of sun hit a puddle

and a distant radio told the news. I saw
a winter tree and then eternity trembled
and my fingers smelled of garlic from before

and the window was smeary, the tea cups
wanted washing and the Gulf Stream
was slowing and O my hips

ached from sitting. My brain's not right,
really:
its latent inhibition so way out

that even a hangnail thrilled;
I was drowning in possibility
while underneath the world

an ice shelf collapsed into the sea
and a cat with a white-tipped tail
walked by and somewhere in my body

the changed cells gathered
and my hair was damp on my neck
and I prayed to be disturbed

and hurricanoes whirled and hissed,
my nose itched, my ears hurt,
and then there was this.

Stargazer

If I'm not looking at you,
forgive; if I appear
to be scanning the sky,
head thrown back, curious,
ecstatic, shy, strolling
unevenly across the floor
in front of you, my audience,
forgive, and forget what's
happening in my cells.
It's you I'm thinking of
and, voice thrown upwards,
to you I'm speaking, you.

I'm trying to keep this simple
in the time left to me:
luckily, it's a slow
and selective degeneration.
I'm hoping, mainly, to stay present
and straight up despite
the wrong urge that's taken hold,
to say everything, all
at once, to everyone, which
is what I'd like if only
I could stay beyond this moment.

Procedure

This tea, this cup of tea, made of leaves,
made of the leaves of herbs and absolute

almond blossom, this tea, is the interpreter
of almond, liquid touchstone which lets us
scent its true taste at last and with a bump,

in my case, takes me back to the yellow time
of trouble with blood tests, and cellular
madness, and my presence required

on the slab for the surgery, and all that mess
I don't want to comb through here because
it seems, honestly, a trifle now that steam

and scent and strength and steep and infusion
say thank you thank you thank you for the then, and now

Piss Flower

I can't pretend to a golden parabola,
or to the downing of many pints
for making magnificent water.

I can't begin to write my name, no
not even my pet name, in the snow:
except in pointless unreadable script.

But I can print a stream of bubbles
into water with a velocity
you'd have to call aesthetic.

I can shoot down a jet stream
so intense my body rises
a full forty feet and floats

on a bubble stem of grace
for just a few seconds
up there in the urban air.